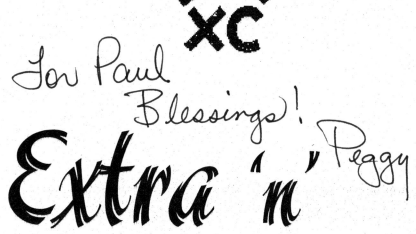

For Paul
Blessings! Peggy

Extra 'n' Ordinary

by
Peggy Godfrey

MediaChaos

Crestone, CO

Peggy Godfrey
19157 Cty Rd 60,
Moffat, CO 81143

ISBN 0-9644375-3-8

Acknowledgments

Vince Hovley, S.J. is an artist who captures the extra and the ordinary all together in his photographs. When this book began to take shape, the cover photograph kept coming to mind. It had been almost a year since I had last seen it. Thank you, Vince, for your observant eyes and generous spirit.

Shahna Lax, whose friendship and gifted teaching are vitamins and minerals for my soul, is my source for all references to the Hebrew language. Below the surface of many of these stories and poems rest ruminations of her insights and teachings from her mystical tradition.

David Nicholas, a most extraordinary poem and story shepherd, has taken little piles of papers and fashioned them into *Extra 'n' Ordinary*. Thank you for giving yourself completely to this work, for your wisdom in bringing order to my chaos, for your words of encouragement, for being you.

Acknowledgments wouldn't be complete without saying how very important you, my family and community, are to me. Apart from you, who touch my life with your presence, phone calls, letters, visits, conversation, working relationships, and play—what a barren wasteland my life would be without you.

Contents

PART TWO

Part One

Extra 'n' Ordinary

Introduction to Part One

Mom has a way with animals," one of the early affirming voices chirped. All the baby manta rays swam to the side of the pool where I stood to admire their unusual shape and ability to navigate. I probably spoke softly to them as I lingered there. On my fortieth birthday the wild mallard mom waddled up from the pond with all nine of her nearly-grown kids to stand at my feet quacking as if they'd done this every day of their lives.

My older son commented, "Gosh, mom, I think they're singing happy birthday" and I knew it was true. Then there was Left-Hind Duck from one of those years when the momma mallard and all her well-practiced fledglings flew out with a passing group of migrating ducks in the fall. I thought them all gone til I nearly tripped over Left Hind as I was cutting firewood. The running chain saw, my location fifty yards from the pond, all his former experiences totally devoid of human contact, and now he chose a close encounter of the out-of-species kind rather than loneliness. For two weeks he trailed behind me fearlessly in the yard, garden, driveway. Then when it was time, he flew. I was never the same person again. Over the years a number of these sorts of events have accumulated; the warm joy and wonder of the original encounter wells up in the remembering.

My desire to write a book of animal stories comes from the warm responses of those who have heard me tell them--many folks whose fast-paced urban lives have cut them off from out-in-the-country childhood memories, others who have no rural experiences to recall, and men and women whose own stories are stirred up to the surface by my stories.

Extra 'n' Ordinary

Wild Raspberries

Roads, trails, cabin sites, logging areas
Everywhere the soil is disturbed
Nature sends her ground-keepers:
Thistles, fireweed, asters—
Known to most of us as "weeds."
My favorite companion of change,
Wild raspberry, likes altitude.
Deep reddish-purple fruit
Hidden in brambles, small and tart
A whole box of the garden variety
Can't equal the intense flavor
Of one ripe wild raspberry.
More than a delight to my eyes
Or a welcome treat for a saddlebag lunch
You tickle my senses
With tender beads of berriness
Your fragrance lingers
In my hands and memory.
Your presence is a promise
That eventual fruit
Can be borne
At sites of disruption
When my altitude is right.

In the 1970s I purchased a honey-colored heifer, a dairy calf to raise on my milk cow. I named her Barbee because of the dairy's brand on her heft hip. As a yearling she summered with my cattle in New Mexico high country and took a fancy to locoweed. Since she'd had a non-lethal dose, she survived as a scruffy and goofy yearling, but lots of yearlings qualify under those descriptions quite apart from locoweed! Except for a lingering disinterest in herd social behavior, she recovered a healthy cow appearance, calved and mothered normally for several years.

One late fall while I was out among the cattle I noticed a few mouthfuls of very chewed green grass lying about--what I would expect the ruminating cow to be chewing and swallowing but not dropping out of her mouth. Okay, something's wrong--but what? As I eased among the cattle, Barbee stepped closer and closer to me. Her large brown eyes held me in a way quite different from usual. It seemed odd but I felt that it was she who had left the green clues lying about. There was no sign of ill health--her nose and eyes were clear and clean, no evidence of scours, no respiratory distress, nothing but that approach and gaze which were out of nature for her. I put several of her companions with her into the corral, called the vet for an appointment, loaded her in the trailer, and took her for a checkup.

Trying to explain why I was there didn't cross my mind until I arrived and all I could think to ask the veterinarian to do was to check her for pregnancy ... which he did. His response was: she is about four-and-a-half months pregnant, but she has a number of nodules, tumors on her cervix and the walls of her uterus. It is very likely that the largest one on her cervix will grow at a rate that will prevent her from a normal delivery when her calf reaches term. In talking with him it was determined that this is one of the latent problems of locoweed poisoning. His suggestion was that I sell her immediately, which in my mind would be unfair to the buyer. I asked if the tumors were all over her body and he said they usually are confined to the reproductive organs. I asked about the safety of eating the meat from an animal in her condition. He assured me that the carcass would not pass inspection if it were unsafe. So next I called the slaughterhouse and made Barbee's appointment.

To describe the unfolding of these events seems a heartless rendering, but the deeper story includes for me the return of life to life, gift to gift. There was no wasted life, no ultimate loss. The one for whom life was no longer an option gave herself in a most mysterious sequence of events to the one who had chosen her and provided for her throughout the years. There was, in the gift of many meals, our reciprocated gratitude.

What Now?

A dog got in with my sheep
  a small bunch doing yard work
  in town
Only two ewes remain in the pen
One, head lowered, bloody and chewed on
Three skittery lambs remain, not theirs
The rest jumped the fence
Ran every direction
Blood, fear, panic
I arrive
Oh, God, what now?

        Walk the streets, yards, vacant lots
        Shake a bucket of corn
        Call to them over and over
        Call to your ewes, your lambs
        If they hear you
        They'll remember who they are
        Whose they are

        And that pull back toward the others
        As ancient as their species
        As strong as breath and heartbeat
        Will draw the flock together
        One body

        Walk slowly, call to them
        Your voice they remember from birth
        Shake your bucket
        Keep walking and calling
        Maybe they'll hear
        And remember

Raising Sheep In Colorado

Ten years ago in late winter I was hired as a day worker to help with lambing on a ranch north of Moffat, Colorado. Scott Selee, the shepherd/herdsman introduced me to life among sheep. A falling-apart copy of one of his books accompanied me home one day early in my employment; it was called *Today I Baled Some Hay to Feed the Sheep the Coyotes Eat.* In it were pen and ink drawings of ewes, a few lambs, but lots and lots of ewes.

Most vivid in my memory were his words that nothing is more beautiful than the freshly shorn ewe. I was NOT a sheep person and the wooly cuddly-looking critters had an interesting appearance, but I balked at his shameless admiration of the naked sheep.

Shearing usually precedes the late-winter or spring lambing for several practical reasons: ewes will be less likely to lamb in a snow-bank without their wool, lambs can suckle successfully when there is no wool in the way, wool quality (cleanliness and fiber integrity) can be affected by the stress of labor and birthing, and a shorn ewe reveals the presence of external parasites, her body condition, and the likeli-hood of multiple births (affecting management.)

Today, with a catch in my throat, I watch my own ewes being shorn--eager to see the beautiful curves of their bodies once again. The lithe yearling ewes even with swelling bellies and udders are no match for the loveliness of those older, deeper, fuller bodies I have grown to love. Motherhood has changed them year by year. What I love most now--along with the author of that ragged copy I read--are those deep-bellied mothers whose bodies can consume and assimilate large quantities of feed into milk for her two or three, sometimes four, healthy strong lambs. My eyes and heart are becoming a shepherd's eyes, a shepherd's heart.

Finding Treasures

In 1991, I agreed to babysit a friend's five-year-old son while she took all-day tests on the Colorado State University campus in Fort Collins. Cody and I left his mom at her testing center and set off to explore. One of my favorite activities is one children enjoy--searching for treasures. I didn't define "treasure" other than by giving an example of coins. Throughout our time together I identify treasures and the term begins to take on meaning for the new treasure hunter. Cody found a penny and a nickel during the first hour with a little coaching from his more seasoned treasure-hunting friend.

We noticed campus maintenance men digging up the flower beds which contained some yet-beautiful chrysanthemums. I suggested we might get some pretty flowers for his mom if we asked one of the gardeners. The fellow was not only happy for us to pick the best flowers, but also spent a few minutes admiring the coins and leaves Cody had collected. As we left I told Cody that the friendly man was also a treasure, but since he wouldn't fit in the treasure bag (Cody laughed) and had work to do, we could remember him as a treasure.

Later in the day Cody and I saw a squirrel only a few feet from the sidewalk. As Cody darted toward it, I noticed the squirrel watched but didn't move. Calling Cody back, I explained that I thought the squirrel was sick because healthy wild animals run away from people. We watched the squirrel a little longer; then I suggested we find a campus security police to tell. No one would get hurt and the squirrel could get help. It took only a minute or so before we located a patrol car and explained our find. She followed us to see the little animal before she radioed for the animal control officer. Cody and I were both interested and decided to stay. As students slowed to look, Cody offered an explanation of what was happening. When the second policeman arrived and checked things out, he quietly told me the squirrel appeared to be poisoned and would need to be put to sleep. He suggested I take Cody away rather than upset him. I asked the man if he would be willing to explain what he was doing and why so that Cody could decide for himself about leaving. He agreed to tell Cody.

In a gentle and touching farewell to the small creature, two generations of strangers honored the end of a life. Cody and I wept quietly. I explained that sometimes, even when a person is doing what is right, it feels sad. As the police left, so did we. I didn't belabor the moment with words, but I know this kind of experience is a treasure, too.

When Cody reported his day to his mom, it was evident that he had valued the emotional wealth of the squirrel experience as much as any of the others.

Weeks later his mom told me Cody is an avid treasure seeker. In fact he found two one-dollar bills at a laundromat full of people, to her utter amazement. No wonder the Scriptures admonish us to "become as little children" to enter the Kingdom of Heaven.

Old Dogs, New Tricks

In January, 1997, Toby and a car collided during a snowstorm; he was killed on impact. Neither of my two other dogs cared much for Toby since he was the new kid on the block, three times bigger than either of the others. He had his own work and didn't fraternize. When the sheep were in the home pasture, Toby spent the nights out at the end of the driveway, barking in response to nearby coyotes. I appreciated his distant barking--unlike Dingo, who finally stopped barking under my window after a few sharp reprimands (years ago), but continued to bark her guardian bark from the yard.

A few nights after Toby's death, I heard a distant barking that sounded awfully familiar. I opened my window to the winter night and listened. Dingo was out at the end of the driveway, barking at coyotes. Though she is losing her sight and hearing as she enters her thirteenth year, she has continued for the past two years to stand sentinel in Toby's place at the end of the driveway as the occasion presents itself. Her breeding has gifted her with qualities which have made her a very useful stock dog; it is from somewhere else in her personality that this aging dog has learned a helpful new behavior from another critter she wasn't even fond of.

Prayers of a Guard Dog

Large white guardian of my small flock of ewes
Deep "woof woof" echoes across the silent valley
Toby's on night watch
Stay away coyote, stray dogs
Dog prayers accentuate the borders
Of a well-marked territory.

Dancing excited playful circles
When my truck passes by his flock's pasture
Following as far as the hay yard
He sometimes waits atop the haystack
For my return from work or town
Then accompanies my truck and trailer
On our feed detail—neighbor's cattle
My cattle and Toby's sheep.

Now we're lambing
I watch to see how he will forge his bond
During this, his first solo lambing.
His movements alerted me to the first birth
A deep woof woof in the night
While I checked heifers
Was his prayer for the ewe in early labor.
She licks her lambs, then Toby's nose
Then back to the lambs.

Oh, perhaps I've gone too far
Calling these dog gestures "prayers"
But calling out the shepherd
Dancing for joy at moments of recognition
    and togetherness
And openly proclaiming my limits
Are my most frequent prayers. 2:00am 3/26/96

In December 1993, my friend Kathy Glenn was ordained to the priesthood. I'd looked for a shepherd's "crook" to give her and none of the stockman's supply stores had what I wanted. As I sat with my disappointment, a very familiar voice said, "Give her some 'shepherd things.'"

Shepherd Things

A shepherd's staff is an extension of the shepherd's reach so as not to frighten the sheep. The very young can be pulled to safety with the mother following, or one animal can be singled out (and caught) from the group without too much disturbance.

Lots of sheep go where the shepherd wants them to go just because they trust the shepherd. The rest go along so they aren't left behind. Sometimes one stays behind because it isn't paying attention. The straggler gets sorta nutty when it realizes it's alone.

Mean sheep are a nuisance so I usually make sausage out of them.

I don't understand why lambs born and raised in the flock can be as wild and flighty as new sheep brought into the group.

Healthy sheep are prolific.

Keep watch.

One of my big weaned lambs survived a coyote attack, even with a punctured windpipe. Trying to shelter her, I confined her in a home corral and provided her choice hay and plenty of water. Instead of returning her to the flock after two or three weeks, I decided to wait. Whether from a lack of companionship or a mineral deficiency, she weakened and could not stand up. Eventually I shot her to end her slow demise. I had done what I thought was best and it killed her. There are some things that I've learned the hard way. I cried a lot.

I lamb in March and April. Sometimes when it's very cold and I've been out for a long time, I hug my ewes to warm my hands and face. On extremely cold nights I blow-dry newborn lambs on my lap with a hair dryer while the ewe sniffs and licks along with me or looks after a twin. David, the shepherd poet, would be proud!

Sheep die, even little ones. And it's never the ones I wish were dead.

Some coyotes kill and eat sheep. Some dogs kill sheep for fun. Predation is when they go for the throat and eat the kill; decimation is when they rip out their guts, then leave the dead and dying, for the sport of it.

All kinds of sheep have wool, milk, and meat in differing quantities and qualities. Appreciation of diversity and potential helps a shepherd make the best decisions for the flock.

Having babies doesn't make every ewe a good mother. Some come around with help. Shepherds get to be surrogate mothers or they may graft a lamb to another ewe. Lambs need milk, love, and companionship to do well.

Keep watch.

Shearing is both a harvest and an opportunity to examine closely for disease, parasites, and body condition. Freshly shorn sheep are vulnerable to snow, rain, wind, and sunburn for a week or two. Make shelter available and they will be fine.

The time just before and after lambing is tough on ewes, especially in a harsh climate. Extra energy from a supplemental food like corn, in addition to high quality hay, makes good sense.

There are several ways to get sheep to do something.

Some of my sheep watch and listen for my truck. If I slow down on the road to look at them or turn into their pasture, the leaders will bring the whole flock to me.

Being a shepherd is an enriching experience and hard work sometimes.

Putting an oily predator repellent on the ewes and lambs is a pretty good way to reduce losses.

Keep watch.

Sheep will eat and do well on a wide variety of grasses, weeds, and shrubs. They can get fat on things that kill cows, and pig out on things that other animals refuse to touch. In fact, they do well just about everywhere.

What you "know" works best if you leave plenty of space in-between for silence.

Musings of
a post-conventional resolutionary

Oh, God,
  Creator of ostrich and avocado
  Porcupine and Episcopalian
Grant me
  The grace to appreciate Your wisdom and sense of humor.

Amen.

To Resolve or Not to Resolve

Can eagle speak for meadowlark
Can mouse speak for ladybug
Can coyote speak for frog
How best to honor God?

Eagle speaks of sky and cliff
Meadowlark speaks of flower and daysong
Mouse speaks for nooks and crannies
Ladybug speaks of green
Coyote speaks of blood and play
Frog speaks of water

The broken and captive sing songs of sorrow
Freedom sings her own song

And none of them make resolutions.

Noah Days

Some days I feel like Noah
Might have felt
When he started cutting trees
For the ark.
My life has direction
But my day doesn't appear so.
There's no "finished" work
And some days I'm busier sharpening my saw
Than felling trees.
Who would know whether I'm cutting firewood
Or starting a lumberyard or toothpick factory??

I have lots of Noah days.

Let's Craft Our Unity

Shall we create a vessel in which
    Our anger and confusion
    Our fears and sorrows
    Our death and life
    Our praise and joy
Can be prayerfully raised to God?

Nectarine Meditation

I am the God of over-ripe fruit
Who will teach you how to gently ease
Each individual away from its soft neighbor.
Never judge by appearance or blemish
Instead, pare away rot and mold.
Then taste how sweet the meat.
Now you know a new way of seeing
For not one fruit in three crowded boxes
Was a total loss.
I am God of over-ripe fruit.

(Just before going to perform for a group of women in Alamosa, I ran into City Market to get eggs. The produce man was "editing" the nectarine display and I asked if I could buy a few of the marked down nectarines. He asked if I wanted all three boxes ---at one dollar for each box.)

In December of 1994, a fifteen-year-old runaway girl showed up on my doorstep. Years of neglect and abuse left her extremely needy but hungry for many of the simple experiences of life. She was with me for two years. Though I wrote this after the first year, I was embarrassed and ashamed to tell anyone but my two closest friends.

Confession

I'm tired
Of not being alone
Having a constant vigil
Of being the always-burning candle.
I'm weary
Of well-doing
Never having a day off
Of feeling like I've been commissioned
With the duties of the Holy Spirit—
   "Lo, I am with you always"
Without having the grace to be holy
   or spirit either one.

Even cowboys get to turn out the dogies
After four or five months.

Meditations

I am the God of the 100th lamb
Not with the flock and in some sort of jam
I am the God of the 100th lamb.

I am the God of an odd kind of gift
Shaped like a problem, too awkward to lift
I am the God of the funny-shaped gift.

Dogies

I've lost count of how many times
Some milk cow of mine
Got saddled with the chore
Of raising another cow's calf—
   a twin, a hungry or poorly-mothered "orphan."
Occasionally a cow would just give in
   after a few days.
Most had to be supervised.
Now someone else's nearly grown baby
   is bawlin' Mama at me.
You don't smell like my babies smelled.
All those coerced motherings are coming back
   to haunt me.
Not that it hurt the cows or me either one
And not that I'd change what I did,
It's just that now I see it differently.
I think now I'd milk the cows and feed the calves
   from a bottle.

If God Is the Fire

During the Sunday morning service I tell the children a story sometimes about sheep, other times about something I've seen or thought about. It's on my mind all week and I approach this time prayerfully. On December 5 when I got up, I put my kettle on the stove to boil water for tea; then I opened the wood stove to build a fire. A cedar log from the night before gave me a few hot coals to work with. As I put some kindling onto the coals I said out loud, "I sure do like to build a fire from hot coals"...the alternative is a cold bed of ashes. No sooner than I'd said it I felt a voice over my shoulder say, "Yeah, me too." Thus my story for the morning worship service began to unfold:

If God is the fire within us, how do we "feed the fire?" Children offered several suggestions--kind deeds, prayer, caring for others. We talked about studying God's Word and worship as other fuel for the fire. One fella suggested "firestarter" which had the congregation chuckling out loud. I told them about my fire-starting effort that morning and how I'd realized that God doesn't like a cold heart any more than I like a cold hearth. If we want to bring God's warmth (love) and light (truth) into the world, then we need to keep a good fire burning.

Well, early in the next week I went to Susannah's to select candles for gifts. She's an Opelousus, Louisiana gal who's been in the west for a number of years, the last fifteen of which she's been creating candles, along with other work. She loves what she does and her house is always fragrant with her candlemaking. I love watching her cut shapes, pour, cool, pour again, do other candle-maker magic, un-mold, smooth and finish her candles. She showed me one of her newer projects --recycling old used up candles which she melts, colors, adds straw to, and pours them into cowpie molds!! Her philosophy is "Nothing is wasted." They are bagged with colorful labels as Buffalo Chips, firestarter. She'd made some red ones for the holidays but they didn't have the right look so she had them ready to remelt. I told her I'd love to buy them for the next children's story--so she gave me some and sold me some and I checked it out with our priest before decking the nativity scene out with awfully realistic cow droppings in both red and brown. Well, now, isn't it true that with God also "nothing is wasted??" The children, after the story of Susannah and her candles and recycled wax, gathered up the cowpies and we bagged them for everyone in our small congregation who builds fires in their stoves or fireplaces at home.

My next story, or sometime soon, I plan to take a few candles and remind the children that candles are made to give light. They can be used for decorations, book ends, dust collecters, or to give away as gifts, but they were made to burn. When God sets us on fire, we give light--and there is a fragrance about our lives which is expressed as personality. For whom do we burn? And I have to admit that I always check out Susannah's shelf of "seconds." These are candles with dips and dents and an occasional unfilled crack among the shapes and layers, some have dings from falling, others have imperfect color-effects; for some reason they don't measure up to Susannah's ideal, so she sells them at a discount. They remind me of me. Dings and imper-fections marring the original concept, but with a perfectly useful wick, they burn with a perfect fire, and the scent is undamaged.

In the Episcopal church we celebrate Epiphany on January 6—a celebration of God's manifestation to the Gentiles (Magi), the out and out declaration that the light of Christ is for all nations. The word "epiphany" is used often to express sudden insight or enlightenment, something formerly hidden "dawns" on us. May we, by the grace of God, burn with brightness and fragrance to His glory.

Who sees the butterfly fluttering
Behind the slatted fence
Unless one loves to glimpse truth
Rather that pin it to cardboard—
Mount and frame freedom's corpse.

God Has Been the Woman

Who comforts me when no one else is near
When pain is so sharp, breathtaking, that I can't even say
    where it hurts
Sings me lullabies during nights when I can't rest
Holds me gently in Her vast silence when I need
    gentleness and quiet
God has been the woman
Who takes my hand and leads me from girlhood to
    womanhood
Holds the mirror as I readjust the image
    of who I thought I was
    to who I am
Who midwifes my dreams, cuddles my creations
Coaxes me to try new recipes for everything
God is the woman
Who builds little fires in the cold rooms
    to warm me to the idea of living
    all the way out to the edge of my skin.

This poem was a 4:00am awakening in response to a "call for manuscripts." Three women who edited an anthology of "women writing from the heart of the West" (*Leaning Into the Wind*) are preparing to do another anthology. They have asked us to submit poems and stories about our relationships with women and made a number of suggestions about possibilities. For nearly three months I've been ruminating on this.

Not Your Usual Night Light!

In the early 1990s I was hired for night calving by a ranch three miles north of where I live. There were nine hundred first-calf heifers bred to Simmental bulls, a rather large breed of bulls to use on heifers. For the first few nights the whole herd stood up and shuffled around nervously in the dusty corral every time I'd walk among them with my flashlight checking for heifers in labor. Those were moved to the more protected area of the lighted shed, into pens where calving problems are more easily managed. Wind and snow aren't as much of a problem for the newborns in the shelter of the shed.

A couple of weeks after I began, I learned that the fellows on the day crew only worked the cattle from horseback. After days when cow/calf pairs were sorted off the "drop lot" group, I'd come to work and find a pretty nervous bunch at night. As I walk through livestock, I talk softly or sing little songs so the stock know where I am and learn to recognize my voice.

Long after they'd settled into the regular two-hour checks, one middle-of-the-night check revealed a very nervous heifer in labor. She'd frantically walk over other heifers, lie down in a flustered heap, sprawl out in the posture of hard labor, then leap to her feet and stumble over more of her corral-mates. I tried to ease her toward the gate that leads to the smaller corral and the lighted shed, but she was much too distracted to cooperate. Often an individual prefers to go with a group--that didn't work either.

I hated to get the whole drop lot stirred up, but that's what was happening without much help from me. It was a bright night so I'd even shut off my flashlight to make my presence less obtrusive. After about ten minutes or so with no luck, I threw my hands straight up in the air and pleaded, "I could sure use some help." At that moment the hingepost of the gate began to glow with a white light that extended way up into the night. My first thought was, "Oh, no! Now the cattle will go WILD with fear." But that didn't happen. The nervous heifer turned toward the gate, and as peacefully as an old halter-broke horse, she walked as if she were being led .... through the gate, all the way into the shed. I followed, closing the gate behind her. Details of the rest of the night blend together with that whole calving season.

Over the years I've "ruminated" on that evening's unusual experience. A year or two ago near Christmas I was thinking of the shepherds and their flocks on the hills near Bethlehem when it dawned on me that no one has ever given much thought to the sheep who witnessed the birth announcement. Angels had to remind the shepherds to "fear not." Anyone who has spent much time around sheep knows how little it takes to provoke a stampede. And if the sheep had fled in panic, you can bet the shepherds would have spent days gathering them. My night with a frantic heifer and a radiant helper lent a clue to this mystery. Perhaps only we humans need the reminder from our creator to "fear not."

ਇਿ ਇਿ ਇਿ ਇਿ ਇਿ ਇਿ ਇਿ ਇਿ ਇਿ ਇਿ ਇਿ ਇਿ ਇਿ ਇਿ ਇਿ

Drip Drip Drip
A small pool
Then flow from the pool brimmed over
Streams and rivers gushing
I'm doing magnificent maneuvers on white water
And you're still laughing
That I've finally started to drip drip drip
Love poems after winter.

Partners

I am called to co-creation
Partner with God
In whose likeness
My spirit was made
In the silent, God-ward seeking
Distractions fade
My creativity lets down her hair
I find my own spirit
In a jam session with my Source
Silence in which melody and harmony
Emerge

Middle School

I love half-grown puppies
Full of personality
Overflowing with "try"

No longer round balls of fur
   Now they're all leg and tail
   Nipping playfully with sharp teeth
   Or drooling kisses
   More energy than know-how
A nose for mischief
They can be found at the end of a trail
   Of shredded paper
   Chewed up slippers
Never properly guilty for creating messes
They leap and wriggle for that
   which is out of reach
Life is a game
Everything, a toy.

The Hebrew letter *Giml* means nurturing not for
dependence but for the sake of weaning.

This aching in my chest
These tears, this confusion
And you know how poets are!!
They want a name for everything.
It's been chaos in my head and heart
A struggle to push beyond the tears
And it came to me this morning.
Weaning! That's what it is
The goal of that intimate nurture
Of a loved one
The moving beyond
That life-giving expression of love
To another fullness of love
One where a spirit of adventure
Is free to set the pace
Where wings spread to fly
High and far away
Songs are cast upon the winds
And love returns to love by choice.

Ah, the sweetness of seeing the hope unfold
And the pain of heavy breasts
Waiting for the milk to dry up.

As I was returning home, a neighbor stopped me on the road not far from my driveway to tell me my cows were out. My aging but attentive Dingo watched me drive past in the truck, slowing as I approached the cattle almost half a mile away. Dingo ran down the road, arriving in time to help me put the cows back through the gate.

Over the years Dingo has grown more observant with less unnecessary running about. Working together is something both of us have enjoyed for over ten years. Her trip down the road was in response to where I was, and only in arriving did she find out she could help me.

Spiritual direction is for those whose lives desire attentive presence with God, those who long for observant ways, who seek God in the mundane. It is a response to the one from whose hand we receive life and purpose.

O ver lunch the interim priest asked me a few questions about raising sheep. As much as I love to tell my stories about shepherding, he certainly got more than he bargained for. Then again, so did I. One of his questions brought up an experience I hadn't recalled for a long time, and in its telling, I found new relevance.

David's question, "How do you deal with the sheep you become attached to?"

It took me back to 1991, my first big lambing season of my own, the year I first heard cowboy poetry, a pivotal year in many respects as I look back. That year my only cream colored ewe gave birth to two ram lambs, both shared her coloring. During the warming spring days I'd go sit out among the ewes and lambs, watching them eat, play, rest. The little brownish twins seemed more curious about me than many of the other lambs, and eventually one of the twins would let me rub his ears and body. He'd even lie down next to my leg. Except for bottle-fed lambs, I've never had such an affectionate lamb. As he grew older, I wished he were a ewe lamb; all the wether lambs go to the auction or are harvested for meat. Ewe lambs I can choose to keep and breed. Coming from a good-milking ewe, these twins were among the first to reach a mature size--which means sale or slaughter. As I considered this lamb, I realized that I would be unable to sell him. Other animals over the years have distinguished themselves as "grace" animals and in time, their destiny or purpose becomes clear.

During this same spring I participated in a cowboy poetry work- shop at the firm insistence of a friend who had heard and enjoyed cowboy poetry and assured me that I would, too. At the end of the all- day workshop, the director of theater at the college where the work- shop was held pulled me aside. She told me that she really liked my poetry, thought I had a lot to say, and wanted to work with me a few times on my presentation because she felt I'd be "going places" with poetry. She explained that people hired her to do this very type of coaching, but that she did not want any pay from me. I was stunned, pleased, encouraged, and willing. At the semester's end, as she suggested, I called her and we met each week for an hour--maybe four or five times altogether.

At the last session I asked her if she liked lamb. She said, "Yes, I love it but can't afford the prices in the grocery store." I told her about the grace lamb and offered it to her.

In telling the story to David I was touched by his pensive attention and his remark, "There's a lot of theology in that story—the sacrifice—can I get you to tell this story in church sometime?"

On my hour-drive home I thought over the story again. The specific purpose of the beloved lamb was sacrifice; and it was my special bond with that affectionate creature which permitted him to be the gift. I, too, snuggle to my shepherd, desiring that closeness more than life itself. And I am aware that in my choice I have relinquished my claims to one destiny--perhaps I shall be a gift, another grace lamb.

ジ ジ

A spiritual director is not a travel agent for a directee's spiritual journey, just an eye-witness of some sites visited.

Sometimes telling you something
Is like rolling beebees down a mountain
If I don't take myself too seriously
I'll admit to the pleasure
Of watching each one
Roll off into never-never-land
And refuse to be insulted
At all the lost beebees.

You know how it is to crave potato chips,
and after eating a bag, realize your craving
was for salt. Shall we presume or dare we ask
ourselves, "What truth does my longing or
desire embody?"

Prayers are nests
Woven to contain hope
When an idea is fertile
Co-created with God
Do like the birds
Sit on it
When it hatches
Do like the birds
Feed it
When it gets feathers
Take it out for exercise
When it's ready
Let it fly
Prayer is home to hope.

Who's Gonna Be
My Soul Friend??

Grandmother or crone
Facets of the same stone

If it's a milk and cookies ministry
      pee-on-the-fenceposts, "mine" territory
      "been there--done that" one-upsmanship
      intoxication on someone else's pain
      fuel for an orgy of psyche fondling
Thanks, but I'm plenty busy.

If it's like winnowing
      slow dancing
      birthing
      adding yeast
      dialysis
      savoring
I'm in for the duration.

Ditches

As soon as John said, "And they point out the ditches," I felt a gut-wrenching "YES." Over the last few days I've thought about the long-ago experience of driving across a snow-blown pasture in my truck with the neighbor who had called me to come help him get his truck out of a snowdrift. As we slipped and slid through the new snow with old snow underneath, I drove in the direction he told me. All of a sudden we hit a ditch which sent us both into the roof of the truck, dislodged every resting tool, rag, nut and bolt in the vehicle. I looked over at him and said, "George, why didn't you tell me there was a ditch here?" I was aggravated that he'd let me hit the ditch with no warning. He replied, "I thought you knew where the ditch was."

"How would I know? This isn't my ranch, I've never driven across this field, and the snow has blown into the ditch so the whole place is just one flat blanket of snow. Come on, George, how am I supposed to know if you won't tell me!" By that time I was really getting steamed up. He didn't have anything else to say so we just drove to his truck and I pulled him out of the snowbank.

Several years later during a wet spring, he got his truck stuck in his corral in the muck and mud. Guess who he called? Since I'd baled hay for him and had bought an acre of land from him, I agreed to drive my four-wheel drive tractor down to help him get his truck out of the mush. His irrigation ditch was running full, but the tracks showed where the culvert was located so I just steered right out into the water. My tractor dropped into three and a half feet of cold muddy water. I looked hard to be sure I'd tried to cross at the right place--yep, I was right where the culvert was during haying season last fall. Maybe it washed out? Anyway, the tractor died, I was more stuck than he was, half a mile from his corral and about three fourths of a mile from my house—feeling really stupid.

After a few minutes I saw a truck driving slowly out through the pasture toward me, so I waited. George and his daughter, in her twenties, drove up. He got out of his truck and said, "I thought you knew we took that culvert out after haying season last year."

Trying really hard to contain my fury I asked him, "George, how would I know you took the culvert out? You called me to bring my tractor down to help you get your truck out of the corral. I live almost 1 1/2 miles from you by way of the fields, five or six miles if I drive around on the roads. You know I haven't been down through the fields since hay season, and you knew I was coming this way with my tractor. These are your irrigation ditches and you knew the water was running."

I don't remember towing the tractor home, but I do remember that it wouldn't start. After the repairs were complete, I'd spent $2,400 because the water cracked the engine block, and all the guts of the engine had to be replaced. When the tractor was back in service, I wrote my neighbor a letter telling him how much my repairs had cost and that I was no longer available to help with haying season or with stuck vehicles—that I couldn't afford it.

☙ ☙ ☙ ☙ ☙ ☙ ☙ ☙ ☙ ☙ ☙ ☙ ☙ ☙ ☙ ☙ ☙ ☙ ☙

Prayer is a lubricant for life's daily metal to metal encounters.

New Neighbors

Our western scenery's changing
With retirees moving in
And some of them are "ranching"
Which is where this tale begins.

High in mountain summer range
I share with regular folk
There is a "new-age rancher"
And his cattle are a joke.

A Scottish breed best kept on moors
They'd certainly keep it warm
Because their meat is skimpy
But, oh, the hair and horn!!

Fluffy faces, shaggy coats
They really are unique
Horns that stretch like antlers
Though beef production's weak.

And you who can be frivolous
'Cause income's not your goal
Have dealt us life-long ranchers ill
With good calves that you stole.

Without much cattle savvy
And fences full of slack
This gosh-awful bull goes visiting
And his owners can't get him back.

This goofy-looking calf of mine
With fuzz and narrow rear
Is a dwarfy, pitiful harvest
For my good cow's fertile year.

You can have your funny cows
If you think that's so cool
But do your neighbors a favor
And get a normal bull.

You've built your house, bought your cows
And thought that you were through—
If you can't keep that bull at home
Then build yourself a zoo.

As I headed up Poncha Pass Sunday morning on my way to church, looking more optimistically over the wall-to-wall day's events now that I had some unhurried moments of driving time, a poem pranced itself right out into the silence:

I want the blessing which lasts forever
But each day, each hour, each moment
I must bring my empty cup
To the fountain of blessing

I would enjoy nestling into a life-long calling
Yet each day I must bring my empty page
To receive modification, clarity, fine-tuning
For that which is written on my heart

I long to remember the extraordinary moments
The common ones, in which
Your Presence became the bolt-of-lightning illumination
          the long slow rain after drought
          the taste of sweet ripe peaches, strawberries
          the lover's touch
And you give me only enough memory
To bring me back to you for more

I desire to write a poem in which you are visible
Yet a glimpse of you now and then
Is all my heart and eyes can stretch to behold
I return hungry, no, famished for more.

Scribbled into notebook space, onto the margin and back of the page, I watch the road and hope something similar to my thoughts makes it onto the page. I carry it with me into class, then to worship. After Communion, I kneel and hear, "Copy the new poem and give it to Lea Ann (who was sitting right behind me)." This isn't the first time God talked in church to me and I remember once responding "Shhh! We're in church" and then nearly laughed out loud at what I said and to whom!! Old rules die hard.

Sitting on the second row, next to the aisle, everyone walks past me to the altar and I felt self-conscious sitting back, pulling out my notebook and pen and writing, for God's sake, instead of looking appropriately prayerful. Finishing, I folded the paper and handed it to Lea Ann. As soon as the service was over I turned around and offered my disclaimer:"Lea Ann, if this doesn't mean anything to you right now, maybe it will later."

Her response, "When did you know to give this to me?" I told her the above story and we visited for awhile as she told me how this poem expresses what she has "been going through for the past three weeks." A couple of folks came to get Lea Ann to come cut the cake for coffee hour. We went downstairs and there was a gorgeous cake, whipped cream frosting, with the message, "Happy Birthday, Lea Ann."

WHAT IN THE WORLD IS SPIRITUAL DIRECTION?

Yesterday morning I got up earlier than usual to make a dish for the annual meeting potluck, load my car for my five-days-away-from-home week, plus the usual critter chores. When I fed the weaned calves, one of the six wasn't with the others. I looked over by the water tank and called out to give him a fair shot at the alfalfa--no calf. I fed the others then walked into the corral nearby to check the feed bunks to see how much grass hay was left. There wedged upside-down was 450 pounds of black calf, bloating himself tighter and tighter into the already crowded space. Alive!! A rare find in itself. What next? I ran into the house and called my neighbor, Hal, a life-long stockman who cares for my animals when I'm not home. He retired to Moffat nine years ago, still has a handful of cows and works colts. Then I found my pry bar and wrecking bar, with my plan for "what next" growing clearer.

Now that there would be two of us, I wasn't feeling so much panic as I was feeling energized by the challenge of extricating the calf. It doesn't matter if Hal has ever had this same problem, he's walked the same sort of life I walk as a rancher. I value having someone else present to help if I need a hand, notice if I'm overlooking some piece of the whole picture, and cheer me on so I don't go back into panic mode.

Later as I was making the forty-five minute drive to church, I saw how closely this story parallels my perception of spiritual direction. Hal and I live near one another, share a love for the outdoors and animals, respect one another's abilities and willingness to be helpful as neighbors. I trust Hal to bring all of his experience and judgment into situations that may arise while he is caring for my animals in my absence, or when we are working together.

The difference between a Good idea and a God idea is just a little "o." Spiritual direction is trusting the Holy Spirit to make the difference clear.

Extra 'n' Ordinary

Part Two

Extra 'n' Ordinary

Introduction to Part Two

"I am here, I am here, I am life, eternal life" were the words spoken to the lonely dying young woman in a concentration camp .... by a chestnut tree she could see from where she lay. (P. 109-110. MAN'S SEARCH FOR MEANING by Viktor E. Frankl, 1959.) Perhaps it was the nearness of death which gave her the courage to tell her simple story to Dr. Frankl. Perhaps it was freedom from fear.

Much of this manuscript began as the telling of "love stories." As a performing cowboy poet and storyteller, I found myself at a juncture: the day to day realities of ranching were full of people going back on their word, pasture leases selling to urban refugees, legislative sabotage of rangeland producers, poor markets. Rather than bring the negatives into poetry and stories, I chose to remember why I love ranching and bring those stories public. Some experiences are unexplainable in linear, logical thinking. I am the first to admit that one of my deepest longings is to make sense of, or find meaning in, what happens to me. It is a way of digesting and assimilating the energies of "soul food." Responses to my first few performances which included these "love stories" reaffirmed my choice to expose both myself and the experiences. Not all the responses were admiration either!!

In the same way a child may grow up to discover a beloved friend or family member to be a recognized and gifted figure of world-wide acclaim (the same person we have "known" and come to trust), our experience and understanding of God grows as we are willing to accept more.

My sheep, cattle, horses, dogs, undomesticated neighbors (hawks, owls, even coyotes) as well as family, friends, and strangers in my day to day living have brought a delicious variety of experiences. From these I have learned new ways of expressing gratitude to the Source of life.

Cochetopa Musings

Joy is the penetrating fragrance of a newly-made candle
    Whose scent seems alive, permeating space and time
    Enlivened each time its wick is set on fire
Joy is the sweet perfume of just-picked wild raspberries
    Begging to be tasted.

And sorrow? the force of a swollen river!
    I am carved and reshaped by sorrow.
Sorrow is the dampness of a mountain meadow
    Soaked by pre-dawn mists, bent in heavy dew
    Saturated by sudden thunderstorms
        or lingering showers

Is not the fragrance of wild roses
Most sweet in early morning dampness?
So joy and sorrow dwell among us
As partners in a slow dance.

Story of Ewe #2

Some days are just too busy for bad news! That was how I felt the afternoon I finished cutting alfalfa on one of my leases. I'd been gone for two and a half days travelling and performing while the first few acres of cut hay lay drying. With beautiful haying weather, I was eager to finish the cutting. As I worked I noticed a tractor with post-hole auger enter the gate of another one of my pasture leases. A suburban followed the tractor and I thought, "They have a lot of nerve making themselves at home on my lease--as if they own the place." Then it occurred to me that the owner may very well have sold it, though he still had my lease check from three months earlier and hadn't given me any notice of his intent to sell or the possible termination of my use of the pasture. The activity and presence these people and equipment presented was a pretty clear message, but I had too much on my mind to panic. Earlier this spring another one of my leases had been sold and I was given all of two weeks to make alternate plans for three dozen head of cattle--again there had been no communication of intent to sell or warning of the impending loss.

After completing the hay cutting I went to check on my sheep who were doing some yard and weedlot work for a neighbor. It was time to bring them home and in doing so I noticed one ewe who limped badly. Her right front leg was injured and she couldn't use it at all. The walk home for the sheep was about a quarter mile and she brought up the rear. On the following morning I herded the sheep another quarter mile to their day pasture and checked the ewe's eartag. She was #2, yellow tag, indicating that she was five years old--and my records show that she had triplets this year. She struggled to stay with the flock but was clearly winded at the gate. Her return home in the evening was even more of a struggle so on Tuesday I held her back. Another ewe stayed with her as did two lambs, one of which belonged to each ewe.

The following morning the entire flock had gathered at the gate to go out, so I let Yellow Tag #2 go with the group and noticed that her three lambs gathered around her and stayed with her rather than scatter among the others. She was growing more adept on three legs.

As I took the flock out and brought them home each day, I thought how pleasing they all are in their good health and vigor; but this shepherd has grown to admire the limping lamb who doesn't lie down and quit and the crippled ewe who won't give up the company of her peers. A deep appreciation for them overcomes me as I admire the spirit and determination, which from experience I know is not a given--for some animals will give up and lie down to die long before their time. I think of myself and how willing I am to be gentle in urging, patient in my expectations for the creatures of admirable spirit.

I pause to reflect on the current sorrows of a friend who has lost touch with his greater community to invest and isolate himself within one relationship. Friendship is one of the precious and intimate extensions of community but not a substitute for community. We lose a great deal when we insulate ourselves from the healthy momentum of like-minded peers--in pursuit of even the most worthy goals. Collective wisdom and life force feed the hunger generated by energy expended in expressing our individuality. Community provides the energy which supports the healing process and adaptation to change.

I look at the enthusiasm and life force represented in this healthy little flock--a pretty lively group to want to keep up with! By the end of the week as I scan the wooly backs of the moving sheep, I would be unable to pick out the crippled ewe except that her movement is a lurch instead of a smooth trot. I spot her in the midst of her community, now quite magnificent on three legs!

Sunday morning they pour out of the home gate and blast away down the road to the open pasture gate. Instead of following, I watch. I think of my week: the loss of these two leases over the past two months means that I am ending a twenty-four year stretch in the cattle business. After my summer and fall leases are grazed I will take to market much of the pride and joy of my life. I've had a leg shot out from under me and I lurch in pain. Phone calls for a summer artist-in-residency and other activities have drawn me away from my thoughts and anxieties. I, too, am feeling the pull to keep up with the dynamic of community, to draw from its strength, its wisdom. Am I going to have the fortitude to stay in motion, hold my place among those I love and admire? Have the timing of this injured ewe and my own unexpected losses come together as another wonder, another story to tell? Will I be able to meet this challenge of change with the same spirit as this five year old ewe?

As I turn to walk back down the driveway, the facts of this parallel story having been my daily companions all week--I hear in response to my question "will I," the cryptic message carried by the crippled ewe's identification. Almost audibly I hear, "Peggy! EWE TWO!"

Autumn Poems

Drought

Pale and sallow
Jaundiced aspens turning
Three weeks ahead of an early start
This early September rain
Is months overdue
Brazen for coming at all
Now that growing season is over,
Irreverent as a platoon
   of drunk bikers
Descending on a small town cafe
   at closing time.
Dry country where water
Is more dear than money
We'll take it whenever, however
Never too proud to stay open for business.

Autumn

Don't give me scientific reasons
   why trees change color in Autumn
Noisy birds spilled the secret
   from my fenceposts.
Trees change colors for poets!
Like breezes that tumble
   ripe apricots in August, leaving them
   slightly bruised but much sweeter,
   the fall which loosens seeds—
Autumn colors, smells, and sounds
   cause ripe poets
   to tumble words.

No Going Back

My childhood home--the deep South
It hasn't fit for years
A beautiful glass slipper
But not my size
I'm kinda like a bonsai tree
Clips have shaped me
Now I grow in odd directions
With so much funny-shaped space
In between

It's not like I'm trying to make it fit, either
But every time I'm back there
For more than two days
I try it on again
Like I might try on an old high school formal
To see if I can even zip the zipper

The Colorado high desert valley I call home
Is my glass slipper
A ballroom where magic doesn't quit at midnight
Where a dream is a wish your heart makes
When you're wide awake.

One morning in the autumn I woke up with my paint gelding, Little Man, right in front of my eyes as if he were standing in my room. All the horses had been turned into the neighbor's alfalfa to graze and Little Man had not come to water with the others the evening before. Seeing him in my mind pulled hard on my heart, so I got up and dressed quickly. I went outside and saw him standing alone in the alfalfa meadow, looking toward my house with his head hanging down. When I walked up close to him, I could see a long, deep, seeping cut across the inside of his back leg. He let me halter him and lead him back to the corral. Little Man was a big strong young horse and had not been handled or ridden as much as the other horses. I was nervous about trusting him, but he did not seem anxious about trusting me.

I called my veterinarian who came over to check the cut and to doctor it. Little Man stood patiently while Marty washed and cleaned the cut, put medicine in it, covered it, and gave him a shot.

My job was to clean the wound mornings and evenings until it healed--a week or longer--and to give a shot each day for the next three days. The gelding's size and strength, and the fact that I'd be alone, made me dread my task. But his clear message that he wanted help and would cooperate wholeheartedly was unmistakable. Each time I washed the deep wire cut and applied the medicine, he stood as calmly and patiently as he had the first time. I never took his sweet spirit for granted. Each time I felt appreciative toward him for teaching me to be still and pay attention. His deep cut could have created difficulties for a lifetime, the vet told me; but instead, it healed so cleanly that one would have to look hard to even see the scar. Ah, the miracle of healing!

A couple of years later I packed Little Man and his mother for an outfitter. We took groceries and explosives way up high into the Sangre de Cristos to Horse Thief Basin for trail builders. Then we'd bring out whatever needed bringing out. When weather forced them out of the mountains, I rode up to pack out as much of the camp as I could. A bear had gotten there first! On the rough and muddy descent Little Man's pack shifted and slipped. By the time I could get him to a level spot to adjust the pack, it slipped down under his belly. As if it were an everyday event, he stood patiently while I unbuckled, un-strapped, untied, and unloaded his gear. This could have been an all-day disaster as anyone who packs animals in precarious places can attest. Instead, we were delayed less than an hour and made a nice day of it.

Sometimes it takes years to witness enough evidence to appreciate the mysterious ways in which life moves to establish deeper connec-tions among us all. Fear is the companion I resist and disdain, yet so often my circumstances require working face to face with it.

Noticed

During the second summer of my ewe-mow lawn service in Moffat, it rained and rained—and rained some more. Putting small groups of ewes and lambs inside wire panel pens, then pulling the whole assembly over to fresh ground when they've cleaned up the first circle has worked well in areas without adequate fencing. I move the pens three or four times each day. On one stretch of ground the vegetation was thick against an old fenceline but sparse elsewhere, so I moved that bunch four or five times a day. Then rains turned the bare ground to slimy mud with puddles in every pan-sized dip. Just moving the pens around muddied up the small patches of grass and weeds. Of course, one pen was at the far end of a really bare area when the rains drizzled day and night. With no hope of a let-up in the weather, I finally decided to pull the panels about thirty-five yards back into taller weeds and better ground cover (less goo underfoot and clean feed.) I pulled and tugged and sloshed and slogged as the dripping ewes and lambs nibbled at the new bits of feed we were slowly passing over.

Working with animals has always been satisfying to me, even with the frustrating and sometimes miserable conditions of our weather. Most ranch work is done "invisibly" as far as witnesses to the daily demands and chores. Many people who saw me in Moffat were surprised to know that I moved the pens every three to four hours and that I gave the sheep fresh water at least twice a day. Folks have commented how lucky I am to get all the free feed for my animals when I "mow" yards and vacant lots and roadways. Not many people ask about the cost of the wire panels, the electric fencing and the solar electric fence charger, five watering tubs for the different groups of sheep, the truck and fuel, as well as the trailer with which I haul the fencing and the animals. Not many people think about the time it takes to repair bent or broken fencing, move the animals and wire panels, get it all set up in a new place, and plan for times I won't be home to move panels. "Free pasture" doesn't seem very "free" to me. All of the people who ask me to mow their yards or the land around where they live have told me they appreciate what I'm doing: cleaning up areas that are a hazard to regular mowing because of metal and wood half-buried in the dirt and grasses, reducing the fire hazard of old dried up grass and weeds, making areas look neat and cared for, plus lots of people enjoy watching the sheep and lambs.

On that rainy day when I moved my sheep over debris-covered muddy ground, I wasn't feeling very appreciated. In fact, I was soaking wet and feeling a bit sorry for myself. No one knew or cared if I did a good job looking after my sheep. Acknowledgment--just some sign that my efforts were noticed--that's what I wanted. Of course, the sheep noticed and in their own way made me glad I'd moved them over onto better ground.

As I walked back to my truck, soaking wet from head to toe with muddy boots, a large hawk flew overhead toward trees on the other side of the road. I looked up and just in front of my parked truck a feather, still close to the hawk's flight path, drifted lazily downward. With time to catch it before it touched the road, I sprinted toward the falling feather--caught it in my cupped hands. It was a perfect medium-sized, mostly white feather with light gray bars on it, still downy and dry.

And yes, I felt like my hard work had been noticed!

Banana Bread

Two loaves I thought were done
A simple toothpick test
Would have told me enough
To leave them baking
Ten minutes longer
Ha! I thought I could tell—
In some cases you can't
Second-guess "done"

Here they sit after a week
My reminder of my thrifty nature
Useless in this waiting
I've sliced the ends to eat
Carved away the gooey center
I keep the other loaf ten, eleven,
Twelve days
Finally realizing I won't want it
Any more tomorrow than today
I throw my failure away
I've studied it long enough
Wonderful ingredients
Botched by my unwise choice.

A Shepherd's Gift

Alayna was an eighteen-year-old, straight-A student raised in the Denver area by her grandparents until her grandmother died--when Alayna was six. Her mother has been in a succession of relationships and marriages. According to Alayna, her mom has a weight problem, drinks too much, and she doesn't get along with her mom. Alayna lives in her own private quarters in her grandfather's large home, which houses both her mother and her mother's mate, as well as her grandfather. When she's at home, she says she doesn't eat breakfast, but eats at McDonald's and Wendy's noon and evening meals.

With no plans after graduation, she thinks she'd like to be a housewife. Her boyfriend plans to join the military after graduation and fly airplanes. He is color-blind, a genetic condition he inherited, which would prevent his being a pilot, but Alayna says "he's getting better." They don't have plans to marry anytime soon.

Last year I volunteered through the Colorado Farm Bureau to host a student for ten days during April as part of a Senior Field Studies program. Designed to offer a variety of life experiences, the program is for students who have maintained a certain grade point average and completed their graduation requirements.

April is a very busy time for me since my ewes are lambing and I need to check them every couple of hours around the clock. I also work mornings on the feed crew at a nearby cattle ranch, the /LD (Slash LD). It seemed to me that the variety of chores and animals would be quite an adventure for a city girl, which is why I volunteered.

Alayna told me about some of the other students who were among the group of twelve being hosted in our large valley. She felt many were too concerned with their hair and make-up to get involved in chores and outdoor activities or too self-centered and stuck up to enjoy being on a farm or ranch. Some of them were her friends.

Since Alayna said she wanted to be a housewife, I figured she might prefer to help me in the kitchen if mornings were rushed. She didn't know how to fry bacon or cook eggs so I showed her how. After that morning she always took longer to get ready and didn't come to the kitchen until breakfast was ready.

For the first three or four days she seemed interested in what we were doing but she didn't ask questions. I like to explain what I'm doing and why I do it, so maybe she didn't want any more information. Every evening she called her mom, and on the fifth day her boyfriend called. He was not having a very good time with his farm family. Starting the next morning, neither was Alayna. There was a potluck the following evening for all the students and host families in our valley, and even though she told her classmates and acted like she was having a great time, as soon as we left, she was sullen and seemed bored again.

In every way I could think of I tried to connect with Alayna who continued to become more and more withdrawn and irritable. On her last full day at my house she was pouty and silent so I asked her if she still wanted to go to dinner at Bob and Judy's. Bob is the ranch manager for the /LD and had taken Alayna to check cows and calves on horseback one afternoon (something she had wanted to do). He'd also taken her with him on some short errands during which Alayna had met his wife, Judy.

That evening at Bob and Judy's, Alayna showed an interest in Bob's arrowhead collection and was pleasant but quiet during dinner.

Back at home we had a new set of twins so I was busy with them for a little while. Coming into the house I heard Alayna crying and shouting into the phone, "Shut up, just shut up! I've been trying for nine days to build a relationship with you and now that I'm coming home tomorrow, you said that. This is the way you treat me every time. Just stop it, be quiet." After another ten to fifteen minutes of arguing and crying, she hung up and told me her mother had started hassling her about not having a job and how Alayna was going to pay for her own airline ticket to a family reunion in the Great Lakes area after school was out. She was really down.

The next morning I dropped her off at the Moffat School to wait for the van which would gather up all the students staying in the valley and return them to Denver.

Straightening the house a few days later, I picked up a bag that contained a small hand-spun skein of wool yarn from my own sheep, hand-knit cap and mittens made with a variety of wools including some of mine, and a luxurious pair of patterned white socks knitted exclusively with wool from my sheep. All the wool had been bought from me the year before, but in order to show off a "finished product," I had borrowed the garments during lambing season to show every-one who comes to my house. The bag seemed light so I looked inside and the socks were missing. Well, I searched high and low for the socks! I'd shown them to Alayna early in her visit, and remembered showing them to the gal who photographed Alayna the day after the potluck. No one else had been to the house. Since they don't belong to me, I'd been really careful to return the garments to the bag so they wouldn't become dirty or misplaced.

Then I knew Alayna had taken them. Oddly enough, as soon as I realized she'd taken them, I also knew why: to show her mom, her grandpa, her classmates, her boyfriend, maybe even her teacher, how special she was that I would give her a pair of hand-made socks knitted from the wool of my own sheep. But Alayna knew the socks weren't mine and she knew the gal who made them wanted forty dollars for them. I felt betrayed.

In detective mode, I set about to confirm my suspicions or prove them wrong. I called Alayna to tell her the socks were missing and asked her to check through her things to see if they were packed by mistake. At least if she had any regrets, she could save face and "find them." She said she'd look. Three days later I called her back to see if she'd found them. "No," she said, "I've looked through everything twice." By that time I'd talked to the valley coordinator for host families who said she vaguely recalled some talk about socks as the kids were loading up the van to leave. My evaluation had reached the state coordinator who contacted Alayna's teacher. When the teacher and I finally talked together, he had just returned from the rafting segment of the semester program. He said he'd asked Alayna about the socks and her response was, "Peggy called me and we got it all worked out. I have the socks she gave me as a gift but didn't find the others she's lost." I told her teacher there was only one pair of socks and I hadn't given her any socks. He told me he'd have Alayna send them back to me. Since she'd lied to me twice and to him once, and since she'd be graduating in a week, I suggested that if he really wanted me to have the socks, he needed to send them to me. He did.

In the process of writing in my journal and talking with friends, trying to decide how to make sense of what had happened, I realized this experience is, in many ways, like another more familiar one.

Among young lambs I occasionally discover a thief: its head will be a yellowish-brown instead of the glistening white of new lambs. Lambs nurse with their heads nestled into their mom's flanks. A thief comes in from behind, often at feeding time when the ewe is distracted with fresh hay or corn. When lambs bump their mother's udder to let the milk down, she usually squats to urinate and defecate. A lamb who steals "gets it" on the head and carries the color and smell long after the theft! When I see a "shithead" in the bunch, I try to find out why. Occasionally the ewe has twins and she favors one, or her larger lamb is nursing both sides of her udder—leaving little or no milk for the other lamb. Sometimes the ewe has mastitis which causes one side to swell and become plugged so a lamb gets no milk. When a baby can't get what she needs from her mom, she steals. Usually the thief is gaunt, naps by herself, doesn't play with the other lambs, and is always looking for another chance to steal a suck or two of milk from an unsuspecting ewe.

As their shepherd, one of my jobs is to separate the thief and its mom from the others. If the ewe doesn't have enough milk, I will feed milk from a bottle until I can sell the lamb to someone who wants to raise a baby. If the lamb is just being a little greedy, I turn the mom and baby out with the older lambs whose moms are more vigilant. That stops her thieving tendencies. Rarely does a lamb steal unless she's really hungry and can't get what she needs from her mom. My job as a shepherd is to help find ways for young lambs to get what they need without letting them do something that will harm another lamb or themselves.

Spring Is Here
When the Drag Is By the Gate

Valentine's Day is barely over
Out come the shovel and gloves
Seeds on racks in every store
For the season everyone loves!

County trucks cruise the roads
A sign that some may trust
But I'd bet bucks that all those trucks
Are political clouds of dust.

The sub comes up in wetter years
I notice when my truck
Begins to sink on dry-looking ground
In which I just got stuck.

One day there'll be some flying bugs
And I'd guess it's gonna get warm
Then I remember yesterday
They blew in with that storm.

Calendars tell me spring is here
The IRS won't wait
Yep, I hear a meadowlark's song
But is the drag by the gate?

Those Swainson hawks that nest each year
In the cottonwoods down in "Three"
Are back. But they're just as cold as us
With their backs to the wind like me.

Breeding season determines the births
Of cows and sheep on a ranch
So babies don't indicate it's spring
Only that there's a chance!

Some folks know when spring arrives
Because they start to sneeze
At the /LD we know its spring
When Skip hangs up his skis.

School's out, summer help arrives
Cattle shed winter's shag
But a better gauge of the season
Is where you find the drag.

These months and months of winter
Seem a mighty long wait
To see the tell-tale proof of spring:
The drag is by the gate.

(In our part of the country a drag is usually made of a couple of railroad irons eighteen to twenty feet long, connected with chains. Potato conveyer chains are welded and wired to drag behind the heavy rail irons another five or six feet. Pulled by a tractor, these drags break up cow manure, ant hills, and smooth down rough and frost-heaved pastures. Dragging is ideally done after the cattle are moved off the ground and before the grass grows much.)

Stories about Vogal Sandlin, My Neighbor
1988-1998

"Did I tell ya about the day I went swimmin'?" Vogal asked me when I stopped by his house one day. He was still doing the irrigating so he must have been 87 or 88 years old. I told him "no," so he proceeded to tell me that he'd gone to the reservoir to turn out the water. He was not wearing his work boots with the rubber-grip soles, and as he walked on the plank out over the water to turn the valve, he slipped and fell into waist-deep water. When he righted himself, his boots sunk down in the mud and he had to work pretty hard to get himself onto dry land. Not wanting to get his truck wet and muddy, he decided to walk to the house. He remembered lots of times he'd walked that far before, but forgot that it had been a long time ago. It was either spring or fall when this happened because I remember thinking how cold it must have been walking in wet clothes. He wore himself out hiking back to the house. He warned me he'd get in trouble if the family found out he fell in—maybe they wouldn't let him keep living there alone. The housekeeper who came in the mornings was horrified and wanted to tell.

One of the warmest memories I have of Vogal was the way he could turn a near disaster into a funny story about himself. He didn't mind telling how cold and tired he got, but always in good humor. He valued his freedom to work at his own pace on his eighty acres.

Then there was the day we were working on the irrigation pipe and the wind was blowing so hard we had to hold our hats and lean into it to keep from losing our balance. He looked over at me and had to holler just so I could hear him with the wind blasting all around us: "if the wind is gonna blow I wish it'd just go ahead and blow!"

No whining, no griping, no complaining. Just a good sense of humor was applied to whatever inconvenience was at hand.

He was in his nineties when this story took place. I'd stopped by and he asked if he'd told me about his truck running off without him. I told him no, so he told me he'd driven out into the hay meadow to see if the gaskets at the pipe joints were leaking. He'd left the truck running and put the truck in park—he thought. When he turned around, his truck was leaving without him, rolling slowly toward the fence about forty or fifty feet ahead. Hurrying toward the open door, he stumbled and fell., knocking the door shut. By now he was getting pretty worried about the truck tearing down the fence, so he scrambled up and made one last dash for the truck, opened the door and got the truck stopped before it hit the fence. After telling me the story, he showed me the bruises on his arms and leg from the fall. With a perfectly good excuse to complain, he reminded me, "Don't tell anyone about that or they'll get worried and not let me drive my truck any more." True to my word, I kept it a secret. He died in October, 1998, so he won't mind now if I tell everyone what a good sense of humor he had!

One summer day when I had my sheep doing a lawn mowing job on a really large weedy fenced-in yard, I took Vogal with me to check on them. My Great Pyrenees guard dog stayed with them around the clock, but I'd go over at least once a day to check the water and feed the dog. As we turned down the long north-south county road, Vogal pointed to an old shed to the northwest and said, "I lived over there when I was a lot younger and I'll bet there are still some craters out in the corral where I used to break horses." We both laughed and he told me he spent more time in the air than he did on horseback some days. His cheerful way of recounting the stories of his life are one of the things I miss most. Not many people I know have so much fun telling about their disasters!

In 1998 I was appointed an election judge at a precinct across the valley (we are a HUGE county), and prior to the August primary election, we had to go for training. On my way out of Moffat there was a roadkill rabbit--which is usually accompanied by various birds, so I slowed a bit. On my return trip I slowed down and passed a huge bird just to the left of the road's center line, sorta splayed out on the pavement. I stopped and backed up, got out and discovered there was not any blood or feathers around, the bird was breathing rhythmically and his eyes blinked occasionally. Oh boy!! He was HUGE. In the sky overhead was another BIG bird with some white under the large wings. This pavement critter was chocolate brown with a tinge of gold—a long orange beak with a nasty down-curve tip for ripping flesh, golden eyes. An eagle. At the time I presumed a golden eagle—though immature (3-4 years old). A mature golden has brown eyes and not so golden a beak. Well, the rule is NEVER handle a raptor without layers and layers of protective clothing and welding gloves, and preferably another person there. I was in a t-shirt and without gloves. I picked him up and checked under his wings (a match with the airborne bird), then placed him in the shade of a chico bush in the grass about ten feet off the pavement—went to the school to call the county sheriff's office who called the raptor rehab in the valley. They called me back at the school and asked if the bird was in a box. With all their warnings and instructions in mind I returned to the bird with a box, a towel, a jacket. I jumped out of the car and started to the bush when I noticed a huge perfectly upright bird about six feet from the bush,regarding me with large golden eyes but no sign of nervousness. So I just stood and watched with my towel in one hand and the box in the other. After about a minute of gawking I said, "You might not be very easy to catch, huh!?" Then my CPR training took hold and I said, "Are you okay?" and took a small step toward this very close and exquisite bird. He didn't flap or flutter but simply lifted himself into the air as beautifully as I've ever seen. After flying a broad semi-circle he flew away. I hurried back to the school to call the fellow at the rehab not to come to Moffat. WoW!! As is my usual practice with an experience like that, I go over it and over it for days and sometimes weeks to see what else is there besides the obvious. All of us have opportunities in our lives to gently move another of God's creation out of traffic lanes into a safe place where they can regain dignity and strength to "fly" again. Why did the story come to me? Because I'm a storyteller and you already know in what ways this experience is true for you also. And why an eagle?? Because it embodies some sort of mystical ideal for most folks and because we need to see without judgement and prejudice exactly what it is we are invited often to do for one another— and the risks.

David

Bag of rags
I hate sheep
He says
As he scoops up a newborn
In one hand
Holds the goofy ewe down
With a firm knee
And lets the lamb suckle
He looks up
With a shy half-smile
I guess hate's not the right word.

One of My Favorite Teachers

Years ago I raised a taffy-brown calf who grew up to be my favorite milk cow. Taffy was part Holstein and part Simmental which is why she became a huge cow, but her gentle spirit was her most noticeable feature. One morning when I went to milk her, as I was situating myself on the milking stool with my bucket between my knees, Taffy slowly lifted her right back foot four or five inches off the ground, held it for a couple of seconds then put it down. I was so busy preparing to milk that I didn't take time to really look at her foot until she slowly raised it again. There embedded in the skin over the ankle bone was a fence staple. Ouch! It was deep enough to sit snugly against the hair with a little blood around the entry hole. I patted her leg to acknowledge what I saw, and told her we'd get it fixed. With very little experience and not much confidence, I was afraid to pull the staple out and risk her kicking me.

After I finished milking her I called the veterinarian, loaded her into the trailer and off we went to the doctor. He gave her a tranquilizer shot and put the nose twitch on to be sure she wouldn't make trouble for him. I talked to her the whole time, but she was calm from the start. After he removed the staple and gave her a tetanus shot, he commented that she hadn't defecated at all--most unusual for a nervous cow. I told him, "She's not nervous. She showed me the staple, so she knows why we're here." I should have added that I was the one who was nervous! He gave me a funny look and said, "Well, you may be right." For as long as he practiced in Taos, he referred to me as the lady who talks to her cows.

Several years later Taffy and the other cows were at summer
pasture, a lease about a half mile from home. It was accessible either
by a winding lane off the main dirt road or across a couple of hay
meadows. After several days on the new pasture Taffy arrived home
by way of the hay meadow with a couple of other cows. I promptly
took her back the way she'd come, tightened up the wires where
they'd crossed over. Another few days later she showed up again with
five or six other cows, this time by way of the winding lane and main
road. Okay, Taffy! She was close to calving so I decided she wanted to
be home for the birth. All the other cows went back to the summer
pasture. A few days later just before leaving with all the neighbor-
hood kids for vacation Bible school, we gathered at the fence to
admire her brand new taffy-colored calf that had just been born. Three
hours later I arrived home to discover a little white-faced red calf
lying next to the taffy-colored calf. No wonder Taffy wanted to be
home!

Moving Toward the Light

Alzheimers is not a particularly light subject, more often not even discussed in detail. Often meanness and cruel accusations are cast by the afflicted upon the lives and hearts of their loved ones who are caring for them. Changed behaviors are explained away, covered up, painfully absorbed but rarely exposed.

My mother quit being mean-spirited toward me when she lost her mind, so these are some of the best years of my life. She never had much of a sense of humor; though it may well have been that she didn't consider it lady-like and rejected that part of herself. I suspect she may have annihilated much of our common ground as women.

Mother currently lives in the moment--not that she has any choice any more. Without connections to memory she no longer has credentials to criticize, humiliate, blame, or otherwise burden the present moment. Neither has she the treasures of memory with which to embroider the current experience upon the fabric of her life. She does however recognize love at a level of her being that is no longer governed by fear and is not damaged by her illness. She can't remember being loved necessarily, but she knows it when it's present. Her eyes say so, her body leans into our touch the way a small puppy or lamb responds to tenderness.

A few years ago on a visit to my parents' home I noticed a sign by the bathtub in my mother's handwriting: "Turn off water." My first response was defensive--as if the note had been left for me. Immediately I realized by the aging tape, it had nothing to do with houseguests! By the phone was a note, "This is NOT the social security office." My parents' phone number was the same as the state 1-800 number for the social security office so they got a lot of calls. In her more lucid moments, my mother made herself cue cards.

After a fall over a year ago in which she broke her hip, mom has been in a nursing home. During her hospital stay, she developed pneumonia. Sympathizing with her, a visitor mentioned how sorry she was about the pneumonia on top of the broken hip. Mother politely replied, "You're in the wrong room, I don't have pneumonia." From the beginning she's never complained of pain, continues to disengage herself from restraints, and tries to get out of bed. One day the air-conditioner plug caught on fire in her room and patients were evacuated from the area. Dad asked her later if that had alarmed her. "Nope, nothing happened here," was her reply. This is the same woman who, in years gone by, got more mileage out of a mishap than anyone else.

For the longest time my dad felt so guilty for putting her into the nursing home, dreading the never-asked question about when she'd get to go home. From my perspective, Mother has come home.

Parasites

Some suck your blood, some eat your skin
Others make you itch
They multiply and fill your space
'Til ya don't know which is which.
They eat the food you ate for you
It's they who gain and grow
And, you, the host, sometimes in pain
Get tired and weak and slow.
Tapeworm 1
Not good enough, the tape plays on
You're just not good enough
No matter how you try and learn
You'll never have the stuff
It takes to quality
Ya have to find a man
Wear his name instead of yours
Get by as best you can.
I'm not afraid of being alone
Of dying or being a nut
My crippling fear--I'm not good enough
But I can't decide at what.
Tapeworm 2
You can't have fun and call it work
You just can't call it work
Health insurance and workman's comp
Are the only permissible perks.
It doesn't count on the real-work scale
Unless it wears you down
Saps your strength, dulls your wit
Makes you grumpy, growl and frown.
You must be serious, don't laugh out loud
Never be "off the wall"
Martyrdom may not be fun, but look
It's your chance to die young and stand tall.

Becoming a Shepherd

Quietly she watched as I raked and spread clean bedding in the lambing shed. When I noticed her standing nearby, having left the flock out on the feedground, I wondered if she might be in early labor. Large twins or perhaps triplets caused her sides to undulate. Well, Missy, would you like to come into the waiting room? She moved through the opened door as if it were her idea instead of mine. That was the year three ewes came in during lambing season, stood silently watching me until I offered sanctuary within the lambing area. All three ewes lambed within two to five hours, all had triplets, and all required assistance for live births—though circumstances differed with each birthing. The last of the three was the longest wait: signs of labor persisted but no lambs came, then feet appeared—upside down. Backwards (breech) lambs drown during birthing unless they are pulled out and jump-started by someone attending the birth because the umbilical cord is clamped off in the birth canal while the head is still within the uterine fluids. Two of the three lambs in that trio were backwards. I remember well that night.

Lambing season was dragging to an end, following two months of calving season during which I'd been working night shift. Three months with cat naps qualifying as sleep, I was exhausted. I'd been waiting for three hours for this ewe to get with it, so I set my alarm clock for a forty-five minute nap instead of the usual twenty-minute nap I allow during labor. My head hit the pillow and I heard distinctly, "Get up and go to the ewe." Give me a break, I was just out there!! Persistently, "Go now." That was when I noticed the tiny black hooves, upside down. Once I'd pulled the little ewe lamb, cleaned the slime off her nose and mouth, mama began licking. I didn't come into the house until everyone was born and talking. The second lamb was a really large male, the third was another little backwards ewe. This set of triplets was the eighth set born that year. Made me think of a poem—eight rhyming lines. And sometimes the last line takes more work, more time than the others. This wasn't my creation but I saw it as a love poem to me. One year earlier I'd had to relinquish one-half of my ewes in my divorce. Before this year, I'd only had one other set of triplets ever. These remaining ewes were hand-picked, my chosen.

As yet another lambing season begins, I remember my very first one ten years ago. The manager was both college-trained and mentored by stockmen; and I, whose experience had been only with cattle, was both apprentice to the chief and jail mucker. "Jails" or "jugs" are the small pens (4' by 4') in which a ewe and her new lamb(s) are confined for the first day so that they bond well. It also gives the shepherd a chance to observe the mother's treatment of her lambs, check her for milk production, make sure the lambs are nursing, and to notice weepy eyes, a genetic trait.

A lamb with weepy eye has an inverted eyelid, which if not corrected will cause him to lie about rather listlessly, not compete for milk with a sibling, and eventually will cause blindness. Lambs who have two weepy eyes frequently won't thrive at all because of the discomfort. Treatment is radical: a clean pair of fingernail scissors is used to trim a crescent of skin from below the eye next to the lashes. As the skin pulls together to heal, it draws the lashes out of the eye. If the weeping continues after several hours, you didn't cut enough tissue away. It's awfully hard to put a lamb through that process twice knowing how small he is and how much he suffers—so it's best to do it right the first time. Usually lambs respond remarkably within 15 minutes, nursing and jumping around as if nothing had ever been wrong. I've been asked by other sheep people what to do about "infected eyes" in lambs. I offer to come over and work a miracle on the infected eye, because the explanation and technique don't fly well to those who hope an eye ointment will fix the problem. This was one of my first lessons in shepherding. Every year I thank Scott silently for this gift.

A ewe's udder has two separate milk factories (cows have four). Mastitis is an infection which closes down the works in one or both sides. Babies may suck vigorously but they will starve to death; ewes will lick and love those babies but they can't raise them. Perhaps the saddest job a shepherd has is to take the one, two, or three lambs away from a mother who bleats helplessly for them. A ewe can raise one lamb if only one side is rendered useless. And that brings us to the "bums." A bum lamb is an orphan from any of these possible reasons: his mom died or didn't have milk (age or health-related), had mastitis, didn't want him and refused all the efforts to bond them, or there were more lambs than the ewe could raise and this was the smallest or weakest of the siblings. One of the reasons a ewe will not accept her lamb brings up the "granny." A ewe having twins or triplets may get separated from her firstborn. Older ewes who are getting close to lambing (or may even be in labor), will take a shine to the little critter and talk to it, lick it, and let it nurse. By the time someone finally shows up to jail the ewe and her lambs, there's some confusion about who belongs to whom. A granny will usually reject the lamb she's stolen once her own lambs are born. That's one of the reasons a shepherd needs to check the flock often during lambing. The lamb's mother rarely takes back a lamb that has been grannied away from her for very long.

A bum lamb can be sold or given to someone with milking goats, it can be bottle raised on lamb milk replacer (much like powdered milk), or it can be grafted to a ewe whose lamb dies. Unless the orphan is arriving at the same time a ewe loses her lamb (the bum can be smeared with the birth slime and smell right to the ewe), then the ewe's dead lamb can be skinned and the skin tied to the bum. Always include the tail on the skin—Moms go by smell and if the lamb has lived long enough to have his mom's milk go through his digestion, she KNOWS the smell of her own milk. Older ewes may be too smart to fall for this—unless their granny instinct is running strong. Milk replacer is a very expensive route for raising lambs not to mention the time required for bottle feeding.

During lambing season the relationship of a shepherd to the sheep is begun, reinforced, deepened, or forged—depending on each year's variety of circumstances and problems. Because sheep are not pets, touching and really close contact are usually reserved for vaccinating, shearing, lambing, and emergencies. Ewes sniff my hands each time I approach the "jail" with food or water. If I need to get in with them to assist a lamb, they may even put their faces into my face to "share breath." Ruminant breath has a shocking sort of smell, but the fragile moments of closeness prevent me from stopping this intimate encounter. It is in these moments I make connections which serve me the year round.

When I first began working with livestock nearly three decades ago, I felt like the most timid preschooler who has been longing for this first day of school to take me to that place in life where everything is all grown up—safe, known, graceful, no surprises, no feeling so stupid and helpless. HA! The secret is that getting on that school bus is the surest way to find out year by year that there is no "getting there" on this bus. Last week in an airline magazine I read about the hectic pace of life and the author admonished his readers to "carpe the damned diem." I think I remember the movie "Dead Poets Society" revived that old phrase, "Carpe Diem" translated "seize the day." Anyhow, in the livestock business there is no "there" that one arrives at. So you better like stories and carpe your own damned diem.

Early one summer one of my yearling heifers crawled through or jumped over the pasture fence into the irrigated hay meadow where there's just enough alfalfa to make trouble. I saw her standing on the wrong side of the fence and hanging out close to where the cows were grazing. When I went for her, I opened the gate and started to take down the electric fence net I'd set up to allow the sheep to graze the bank next to the irrigation pipe. When she saw me, she started walking toward me (which young stock usually don't do!), so I began to walk away and talk to her. My little bunch of cows got interested so they began to walk down the fenceline toward me, too. I dreaded the heifer's 700-pound ballet over the delicate sheep netting (plastic with wire twined in to carry the current), but this was already going much better than I'd hoped. She slowly lifted each leg over the netting, not even catching a hoof on the top strand, and followed me down the fenceline to the gate where she joined the herd who had walked with her the whole way.

I was pleased beyond words by her desire to come home and awfully grateful that she hadn't bloated on alfalfa or destroyed my electric fence (an expensive item) on her journey home. But, regardless of how much mischief she'd caused, getting her safely home was my heart's desire. It's a "shepherd thing." more accurately, a "stockman thing." Part of the stockman's "eye" is noticing and responding to correct or intervene in something that threatens the health or safety of one's own critter or bunch of critters.

Here in the northeastern part of the San Luis Valley we have a lot of soluble salts in our soil. When the water table rises in the spring, up comes the "alkali" and as the surface of the soil dries, it turns white. Irrigating helps send the salts back down below root zone, or wash them off the surface of newly worked soil. Late-season snow and heavy rain cause the salts to accumulate in puddles or standing ground water in lower places. Older cattle and new calves don't seem to have problems with the temptation to sip this toxic brew, but yearlings seem to be able to find a single puddle in 40 acres and drink as if there were no tomorrow. Sadly enough, many limit their tomorrows. Most die.

Sulfate poisoning, or "pasture polio" in the earliest noticeable stages causes an animal to hang out by itself, follow a fenceline, or plod about in sluggish circles. His brain swells, causing blindness and probably a horrendous headache. He quits eating and drinking, so the next most likely thing one notices is that he looks awfully shrunk up and skinny—out there all by himself, drooling.

Last year was not the first yearling I've treated for "alkali poisoning" but he was the most memorable. Once you are in the intimate struggle with life and death, the critter usually gets a name. For reasons of privacy, I will refer to this calf by a fictitious name, Wally. After he was safely on the side of life, ten days after the onset of his death dance, I named him after a friend of mine who'd made some toxic choices.

As I drove past the pasture where my cattle were grazing the end of May, I noticed a red steer hanging out about a hundred yards from the rest of the bunch. Not an ordinary sight except when the herd is scattered out grazing. They weren't and he wasn't. I made a mental note to check him up close on my way home after the two hours I'd be away. I forgot him until I got home and there was a message on my machine from the sheriff's dispatcher, "There's a dead cow on County Road 60 about a half mile south of your place, Peggy, would you check it out?" Yikes! How could I have missed seeing it? So off I went to investigate.

With less than forty minutes of daylight left, I found the red steer on the outside of the pasture, lying in the small depression between the fence and the road, eyes rolled back, breathing, and drooling, with his legs straight as boards kinda thrashing weakly. Yep, he's alkalied. But how on God's green earth did he get over or through the fence?? The wires were intact and the fence was not low or loose. Poor critter. I stroked his head and neck, wondered if angels had lifted him over the fence, and hurried home to hook up my truck and trailer. In a moment of panic I phoned a family living nearby with a sturdy teenage son—he wasn't home. Back I go with three of my ten-foot portable panels, a lariat, a long soft rope, and a rather desperate prayer for help. The calf out-weighs me by at least 400 pounds, and it's nearly dark. I turn the truck and trailer around in a nearby driveway, pull alongside the calf, set panels around him so if he does get up he can't go far, back the trailer right up to his nose by dropping the left wheels into the same ditch he's in. When I got the trailer doors opened out and secured, I looked at his limp carcass and wondered at my sanity. I got the soft rope tied at one corner of the back of the trailer, figuring to run it behind his rump and back through the end pipe on the other side of the trailer to guide him forward into the trailer. The problem was he was not standing up. I sat down by his shoulder, reassured him of my intent to help him, informed him that I'd take care of everything else if he'd just please get up. In moments, he did just that. I lifted one foot into the trailer (ever tried to make a stiff front leg of a 500 pound patient step up about a foot??) and he managed to stagger the other one up with me keeping the rump rope snug. When his hind legs were next to the trailer, I kinda leaned hard on his rump and we tumbled into the trailer together. Gates shut, we drove home. I dipped his nose and mouth into a bucket of water but he wouldn't drink. If he lived til morning, we'd go to the vet. He did and we did. What I realized as I came into the house, by now it was dark, was that I would have been unable to drive the truck and trailer to where he was in the pasture when I saw him earlier. For that matter, over two-thirds of that pasture is inaccessible when the water table is up. Everything will sink and stay til the water table lowers. His "dead cow beside the road" adventure was his ticket to life.

First thing next morning we head over to the vet. Marty pumped him up with gallons and gallons of water since dehydration is already a serious problem. Two medications to administer daily: one to reduce the swelling in the brain and B vitamins. Seems like he gave him some sort of energy supplement, too. But the best medicine I took home with me was the story he told about Ralph Mitchell and his alkalied heifer. Ralph, who died four years ago at the age of 94, was a man I admired. You know how you tend to think that the older, more experienced ranchers don't have the same problems as the younger ones— or that they are luckier or charmed?? Well, Marty and I are the same age and for him to be a vet for Ralph's cattle, the experience had to have taken place sometime in Ralph's seventies or eighties. Marty told me the story as we re-hydrated Wally.

When Marty checked Ralph's alkalied heifer, he said she was pretty far gone. He'd told Ralph, "Every time you come out here, stick some hay in the corner of her mouth and give her something to chew on. If it's in her mouth she'll chew and swallow it, but she won't eat on her own. Stick her face into a bucket of water and maybe she'll drink some, too." A day or two later, Marty stopped in to see how the heifer was doing. There Ralph was, camped out with that heifer, stuffing hay into her mouth hour by hour, dipping her face into a bucket of water—patiently and persistently fighting for her life until she recovered sufficiently to do those things for herself. And she did, too.

As I clipped bucket after bucket of grass and sweet clover from beside the road and everywhere else it had begun to grow tall, I thought of Ralph and that heifer. Hour by hour I stuffed little wads of grass into Wally's mouth, hoping these tasty morsels of spring would stimulate his appetite. After a few days he began to drink on his own: he'd stuff his nose all the way to the bottom of the water bucket and blow bubbles and make the most nauseating mess of his water—but he was drinking some of it. I'd wait til he was done, dump the gunk, and fill it again with clean water. Then he began to eat on his own. After a short bout with coccidiosis, he began to rally. He had a droopy eye and a stiff-legged stagger to his gait, but he was definitely on-the-mend. Wally quit standing patiently when I gave him his B vitamins; a shot with a muscle-tingling dosage. He grew alert and began gaining weight. Soon he was in the bloom of good health, a stockman's favorite success story!!

Ranchers who have good veterinarians are fortunate. Those of us with good vets who have lived in the community for most of their lives and practice story-medicine are blessed beyond measure.

Knowing things—you know, that accumulation of knowledge, used to look like the best set of tools a person could have. As years have come and gone, I'm noticing that seeing things has an even greater value.

The roots of all Hebrew words hold the power of verbs-you can't catch them because they are in motion. ROEH, the present verb from which the word "shepherd" comes sounds exactly like the word for "one who sees" but the spelling in the Hebrew language differs. From exactly the same root as shepherd come the words desiring, companion, friend, take pleasure in, and purpose. As in much of my work with livestock, hearing the seeing is how I get a good bit of my information.

One June, I awakened in the wee hours of morning to hear a lamb crying. Instinctively I knew the lamb was caught in a fence. Startled by the crying, I sat up to listen at my window. Since I'd brought home four new ewes, three with lambs, I had awakened several times in the night to hear ewes and lambs talking to one another. No sound from the sheep. Then I realized I had been dreaming. I heard in my heart, "The lamb is Brooke," whom I recognized as the daughter of friends. A conscientious and bright student, she had just graduated from high school and had become romantically involved with a 45-year-old ex-drug user (very recently clean and sober) who worked at the same place she did. Her parents were frantic, fearing she would abandon her plans to leave for a year in Israel, her ticket already purchased and bags packed.

I prayed and wept for 15-20 minutes thinking of what the analogy meant—the fear, struggle, pain, the giving up, the renewed struggle and pain. Prayerfully I wondered what to do. On my way to church it became clear to me that the message is for Brooke—the giver to be identified as "the shepherd of your heart." I wondered about saying anything at church and was reminded of what I've been reading: we minister as the Body of Christ. So I told my dream in Sunday School and invited the class to join me in prayer for Brooke. Also I wanted to present myself for anointing in the worship service. The visiting grandson of Bob and Marge Smith, ten-year-old Aaron, came to assure me he'd pray for Brooke. I encouraged him to come up during the worship service to pray with me at the altar, which he and his grandparents, and others did.

85

Asking for confirmation of the sense that I should tell Brooke was graciously rewarded with three songs in the service. The first I'd never heard before about being called as one of the prophets, the second was the Servant Song (my world-class favorite), and in the third (How Great Thou Art), I sang Brooke's name out loud in one of the verses. I was totally ecstatic. I came home, changed clothes, went to move the sheep to fresh feed—and found that one of the lambs was out. I moved about doing my chores and at the right moment, grabbed a leg and put him back in: no muss, no fuss. Then I got another reaffirmation that my job is helping lambs stay in the safest place possible. I drove to where she worked and two women told me she wasn't there, asking if I wanted to leave a note. I did, not knowing if or when she'd ever get it since the women told me she no longer worked there. It was in God's hands. As I began to write, it felt the same way poems come; I was to tell the dream, the words that followed, and that the message was from "the shepherd of your heart." I concluded with what my prayers for her would be: that she would allow the shepherd of her heart to free her from the tangle of wire, that she would know how beloved she is, and that once free, she would return home to her shepherd.

Later in the week I heard from a friend that Brooke had contacted her mom, caught her plane (with some last minute kicking and screaming), and was in Israel. A couple of weeks later, Brooke's mom called to tell me that Brooke was settled in and adjusting well to her new home and thanked me for my note which Brooke told her about on the way to the airport. Three months later I received a letter from Brooke saying that she thinks often of the dream I wrote to her, "now it is very significant to me" and "hope that now I'll have my head on straight enough to not follow my nose straight into barbed wire! Actions aren't easy to sort out ... Thanks so much for your 'indirect support'...."

I try to remember how concerned I was that I'd mess things up or not hear God correctly. There was an urgency my emerging shepherd's heart perceived—yet my necessary wait for guidance. I felt foolish. There was no assurance of what, if any, response would follow my "obedience" and there was a natural fear of looking like an idiot, sounding like one, and having all these witnesses who are my friends.

Over thirty years ago, as a newly-wed, living in an "economy" apartment complex in Dallas, Texas, I remember the couple who lived next to us. With paper-thin walls a person knows more than they want to about neighbors, but Pete was a bus driver—city transit. They'd moved from Washington D.C. because a fellow tried to hold up his bus one day and Pete shot him. In one conversation I remember Pete saying, "Ya know, if I'd had a chance to get the education, I think I'd have been a brain surgeon." In the privacy of later on, my husband and I laughed that he would say that. Now I wonder if he wouldn't have been a pretty good one!! In the military my husband, a dentist, had a few patients who asked how they could get to be dentists. He told one fella that he'd been a lettuce shredder and got cross-trained. As far-fetched as it may seem, I feel like I've been cross-trained to something I can't even name!!

Recently a friend of mine was discussing a situation at work and all of a sudden I'm thinking of how my border collie, Kay, works sheep. Hey, I was paying attention to what my friend was telling me, but there was some sort of common thread. I asked her if I could tell her a sheepdog story and she said, "Sure." Every year when the lambs get old enough and the grass greens up, I start herding the bunch down to a leased pasture about a quarter mile from where they are born. Kay's job is to make sure they all go together. In the beginning the lambs stay close to their moms and the moms are keeping an eye on the little ones. As they grow lambs begin to play, horse around, stop to graze, sniff something they see in the brush, and moms aren't nervous about the daily routine. Kay's job now is complicated with all those little self-willed teeny-bopper lambs. Each day brings its own new surprises, but the over-riding rule is to get the bunch moved all together. As part of the flock, lambs will be safe from getting themselves in a jam or being eaten by coyotes. Separated, they become frightened and make more foolish choices. "Success" is not in how quickly they grow into flock-wisdom, it's that Kay and I stay with the job day after day until every lamb learns to watch the others. On occasion Kay will try to gather and move the sheep and they resist her. She moves in closer and ewes stamp their feet or scatter. Sometimes Kay will back off on her own, other times I call her back when she gets caught up in the face to face contest of wills.

One characteristic of herding dogs is called "eye" and it refers to their inner confidence and actual power over the herded animals. An aggressive dog does not necessarily have strong "eye" nor does a timid dog have weak "eye." Kay was a slow developer and seemed totally intimidated by livestock until she was nearly two. When she came fully into her "eye" she stunned me. She works quietly and confidently, gently with sheep, and with the vengance of a woman scorned when she herds belligerent cattle or bulls on the prod. We are partners in the livestock work and I love to watch her work. One of the other characteristics about her that I deeply respect is that she keeps her eye on me for visual and spoken commands. Backing off is not a sign of weakness; it is an opportunity for Kay to regain her power, recapture the bigger picture, and clarify whether she is still doing what I want. Pleasing the person who loves and cares for them is the number one priority for most herding dogs, and is the means by which we stockmen "control" our dogs. Finding ways to communicate what we expect and train our dogs and horses to be working partners is sometimes difficult and slow. It requires that we recognize our own weaknesses and limitations as well as strengths. We must also accept these helpers with their fears, limitations, and gifts. Interestingly, my friend found the dog and sheep a worthy analogy.

New on the scene is Whitney, my one-and-a-half year old Great Pyrenees, who came just before lambing this spring. She is a guard dog which means she patrols the area for coyotes or other threats to the sheep during the night and early morning. Bonding with the shepherd is not essential for these dogs, but they must feel a protective bond with the flock or they won't be effective guardians. Whitney is energetic, playful, affectionate, loves her work, and is the only dog I know who can prance down the road toward the sheep without causing them to turn and stampede in the opposite direction. Her sheep-sized body carries a very different intention than the much smaller herding dogs.

For the past three summers I've been taking my sheep to town to graze yards, weed lots, roadways, and overgrown alley easements. That began when coyotes were eating my profits due to some unwise legislation in our state. I call my summer flock "Ewe-mow lawn service, not a baaad deal." This past summer I had a request to graze a large overgrown lot just south of the town of Moffat. It's over two miles from where I live but not within the safety of town, where coyotes pass through but have not yet attacked my sheep. Would Whitney stay with them and allow me to utilize the several days of feed? She's young, has she developed enough trust in me to work so far from home and stay put? She could easily run with my truck and try to follow me—or even venture out on her own to try and find "home." I loaded her with the last bunch of sheep and when I put her out, I could see she didn't feel very comfortable. What could I do to assure her that I will come back, will feed her, will take her home again? "Leave the trailer," came my response. Each morning and evening I took her regular dog food along with some special nibbles to remind her how happy I was with her. By the third day she wanted to show me her perimeter run—she'd go farther and farther, looking back at me as I watched her. What special moments these were! After ten days the sheep were finished cleaning up the weeds and home we went. Had Whitney not been willing to stay, I'd have brought the sheep home rather than risk losses to coyotes. It wouldn't have made her any less loved if she'd refused the assignment; yet I was aware that if she would stay, our working relationship would move beyond the common. And so it did.

In the social order of daily life, the matriarch of the home place is Dingo—the oldest and most infirm. Second is Whitney, the largest and youngest of the dogs. Last comes Kay, Miss Hospitality to all our guests. Kay has to be chained if I am gone for more than a day or two when there are sheep confined in the trap or corrals close to the house. She can't resist the urge to corner a bunch and hold them there. If it were in response to my command, we'd call it good work; when it's her idea, it is called hassling the sheep. Children, especially, love for me to talk about the "hand of God" training technique. When a dog is doing something that she knows is wrong, and is so distracted that she doesn't notice my presence, I bop her on the head with a well-aimed rock. It is excellent reinforcement to training. If it is used when a dog doesn't know better, it's confusing and much less effective.

Perhaps the best lessons I've learned over these years are that there are lots of ways to do any job, working with the nature of an animal is less work, animals are better at reading "intentions" than they are given credit for, and it's a good idea to use the word "becoming" in reference to your efforts to be a shepherd or stockman because humility comes with the turf.

Times Are Changing in the West

Several years ago my sheep shearer told me a story that I cannot forget. In southeastern Colorado there lived an elderly couple who had spent their lives ranching. Though no longer engaged in full-time ranching, they retained a small flock of forty Suffolk ewes.

Escaping the confines of city living, new folks were purchasing land, building homes and moving to the country. One of these new immigrant families had two large dogs, Rhodesian Reds, which were seen from time to time roaming the countryside. Rhodesian Reds are used for lion hunting and large roaming dogs are known for getting into livestock. They may chase, chew on, or kill stock. Many ranchers simply shoot dogs that come onto their property rather than wait until a disaster.

After seeing the dogs on their property, the elderly couple contacted the new neighbors and asked them to please keep their dogs at home, explaining that no damage had been done, but the potential was ominous. The new folks stated clearly that they had moved to the country so their dogs would have the freedom to run and play.

Some time later, before leaving for town, the elderly couple corralled their ewes who were close to lambing. During their absence the two large dogs got into the corral. Upon returning, they found the dogs amidst the death and dying of their entire flock of ewes.

Within a couple of months the elderly man died; soon after that his wife died. Hearts can contain only so much sorrow.